Split-Soul

Poetry from the Heart

KAREN LANGRAN

SPLIT-SOUL

POETRY FROM THE HEART

By Karen Langran

Transcendent Publishing
PO Box 66202
St. Pete Beach, FL 33736
www.TranscendentPublishing.com

Transcendent
——Publishing——

ISBN-10: 0-9982869-2-3
ISBN-13: 978-0-9982869-2-1

Printed in the United States of America

DEDICATION

In the loving memory of Mr. Dad and any survivors of trauma.

CONTENTS

ACKNOWLEDGEMENTS

To Sue K. --- You saved my life. Thank you for caring.

To My Parents --- You believe in me. You taught me truth. You taught me love.

To Rory --- My precious light. Your enduring guidance… Thank you for finding me and bringing me home. I love you dearly!

To My Daughters --- My inspiration. May God put peace and joy on your path. I love you both!

And to Danielle…wherever you are. For holding my hand and protecting my heart. And for allowing me to speak the truth. There are no words. You saved my life.

To 2 Friends that played music on the phone – you know you helped me through.

And to Char, Kira and Paulini who made sure I got up in the morning. You gave me a reason to keep going.

To Joan---a true friend, someone who knew and understood without any words. I thank you wherever you are.

To My Guardian Angels --- I know not who you are, but I felt your presence at the moment my light went out and the candle kept on burning. You made the flame dance and I was mesmerized. Thank you.

To Shadow --- your thumping brought me back to the present. Your gaze held mine and beyond.

To Barney --- You were always there...Understanding to the depths of my soul.

To Russell N. --- Thank you for not exploiting my truth and allowing me to be your friend.

To Phyllis --- for your grace, love, and support in the making of a new path. I thank you.

To God – for giving me the courage to speak my truth and let it out.

And to those survivors of trauma, your life is worth it.

INTRODUCTION

Dear Reader,

I invite you in to read my poems and be moved by the experience. Sometimes life is *not* fair and can't be justified. However, that pain still stays deeply-rooted in your soul. These poems are a collection of years of work, brought about by my emotionally-charged and highly traumatic, life-shattering events that caused me to have a "Split-Soul."

Rather than let you be swayed by my personal traumas and thinking you can't relate, I ask you to please keep an open mind and see if anything moves you along your healing process as you read. Just remember, you are special—there is only *one you*—and you deserve to be free from the repressing and stuck memories of your own life experiences.

If my poems can shed just one trickle of light or one small glimmer of hope for you, then I will be happy and fulfilled. For in your own moment of darkness, you are lost. Fear clouds our thinking and makes you freeze. But if you truly stay connected to who you are, and "can look in the mirror and know you told the truth" as my Dad said, then you will be at peace with yourself and will start to heal. It will not happen overnight, nor in just a few months, nor even in a few years, but by trudging through the darkness, will you find your own pieces to the puzzle to create a new life. Even though the shattered pieces stay inside of you, they will continue to mend as you breathe and grow. I can only hope to share pieces of my shattered "Split-Soul" with you --- and in so doing, I am fulfilling a personal goal that has been stuck in me for over 20 years.

Thank you for staying open and present; I hope you enjoy my poems.

"Truth brings healing to my soul." (My quote).

Kindly,

Karen Langran

"What lies before us and what lies behind us are small matters compared to what lies within us. And when you bring what is within out into the world, miracles happen."
-Henry David Thoreau

Thank you for picking my book to read and allowing my miracle to happen! I appreciate it greatly!

SPLIT-SOUL

Sturdy yet soft.

Strong yet confident

Pretty and flowing

Inviting everyone in
    to read.

Not just reaching
Survivors like me
but all, who endure
    humanity
trauma. Can place the
words in their head
and get some relief.

Some kind word.
Some moment of peace

Split-Sole
    Like the soles of your feet breaking

Shattered Soul

Like the continuous bonds broken and scattered

Saving Souls

Trying to pick up the pieces to learn from and teach others through our strength

A Way Out

Finding lightness in the dark tunnels and webs of chaos

Breakthrough Bonds

Glimmers of sunlight peeking through the crevices

Trying to Turn My Life Around

Making constant changes

At The Top

Following my mind and spirit

Radiating…Life

Living again

A Wrong Turn

Don't let fear bring you back again.

Go Back!

Look out towards the castles in the sky.

Split-Soul

Radiates into a rainbow of subtle colors.

Simple décor.

Purple and white light

breaking in two.

The Flame That Saved Me

> Angry fire with red and orange split up the center

Burning Soul

> Of white light around the top, like a protective curve or
> invisible shield.

Stacked Up To Break

> Do you keep on climbing into the fire? Your eyes are closed.
> You are too near.

Another Wrong Turn

> Stand back. Create space. Breathe again.

A Complete Turnaround

> Try until the pieces resonate with love.

Seeing The Breaking Light

> It flickers, it adjusts in the darkness, breaking ground; So
> your split-soles will walk together again.

ONE FAMILY

> Allowing your Split-Soul to heal through and through.

YOUR LIFE MATTERS

The rain is constant.

It never stops.

Flowing

Falling

All around you.

Above you. Below you.

Through you.

Why must it keep going?

Change is inevitable.

Not always pleasant.

Not always wanted.

But a constant.

> There.

> Here.

> Everywhere.

Bells ringing. Chiming.

Trying to get your attention.

Wanting you to slow down.

Drowning out the noise,

the chatter amidst the chaos.

Hanging on to a space of peace.

Why must I close my eyes?

What if I don't want to see what is on the inside of my lids?

    To take me back to

    another place.

    Another time.

To show me something different.

Shattered glass.

All around.

Head hurts.

Why?

How come I can't get out from the depths below?

This brick weighing me down.

Heavily.

Down a slippery slope.

A path leading nowhere.

Turn around.

Go back.

One step at a time.

Can you see it?

Can you hear it?

 Way down below.

 Crying out for help.

I see and feel a glimmer of hope.

No—it's blocked.

No hope

No cares

No worries

No one

No where

No how—No why.

Again, coming at me.

This rain.

This moment.

 I am OK.

 I am OK.

 I am OK.

  Thank you.

Calm down now

Fears subsiding.

Reaching into the abyss of darkness again.

Why?

Why must I go?

I was happy here

Don't take me away.

To a quieter place and time.

Where all is still.

Those damn bells.

Changing.

Can't they stop?

This is not music.

It is sound.

It is noise.

It is in disharmony.

It keeps on vibrating.

Getting louder.

Floating on a cloud.

Seeing is believing

Why doesn't it make sense?

Torn apart. Ripped at the seams.

Kindness will abound.

    Emily Dickinson

    a poetess of love

    joy, harmony and

    quietude.

Resonates.

Plants itself in you.

Carries you to the Earth

    the water, the air,

    the fire,

    the breath of life.

Can't quite see it.

Still feel lost.

Life all around

moving slowly.

Steady rain
    falling
    falling
    falling all around.

Like church bells, but
there is no church.

Swirling,
I think I like swirling
In my head there is
movement.

Peace on the sidewalk.
Try to catch up with it.

Out of your reach.
Getting closer.

A new path. Turn around
again to see.

Stuck.
Why does it keep raining?
I've had enough of
this life.
It comes in torrents.

There is no end.

The <u>why</u> will never get answered to my liking.

In a forest, alone.

A breeze on my face.

The sun peeking through,

from above.

Racing to catch another

forest.

Another thought

A glimmer of hope

That sound,

A pleasant ringing

Connecting…

Connection to…

    I don't know.

Stuck.

On the ground.

Drop to my knees.

Ask God one more time,

    <u>Why?</u>

    Why me?

    Why now?

Too scared. No support.

No love.

Choking

    throat closing

I am shutting down now.

Melting like the rain on

the sidewalk.

Those damn bells are happy.

They play a manic tune

They start the day

for the next victim.

We keep living with

this broken heart.

Cracked, torn open to

the elements of life

Thwarted by so many
twists and turns,
black holes, caves,
and tunnels – the worst.

No need to stay here
In depair.

Desperately searching
for something new
to unfold

To sort out my direction

To give me a reason
to stay
to breathe the air.

To let up on this chokehold
of life.
    Constantly tugging
    me to pieces.
    Keeping me buried in
    the rubble.

A trickle of water.
Maybe the rain is my friend.
The sun shines on that
raindrop and it radiates
outward.

It has come to an end
again.
They say there is no
beginning or end.
How come? It doesn't
feel that way.

Gets inside of you
and causes a dead end,
a road block of some
sort.

Always this rain pouring
down.

A new face you can't
quite grasp.
A friend reaching out to you.

Feeling your life matters.

Pick up the shattered
pieces.
    Trim them
    Keep them close to
    your heart.
    Build a wall of protection
    around the pieces.
    This way they won't fall out.
    Even though water can get in,
    tears burn. Tears
    turn to stone.

Another wall.
A bigger one.
Bigger still.

Not ready to fly.
Stay grounded.

Plant your feet.
Your life matters.
Even if they don't believe you,

you can come out

alive, well, honest to tell

you don't need someone

to listen.

    Just a hug   A smile

    I am OK.

CLOSING DOWN

Close your eyes. Just feel
Allow yourself to feel what
you're feeling.

Annoying rain / clanging
coming to the surface again
with all those vibrations and
holds – holds you, stuck in place.

I want to get this over with
Fidgety.
Waste of time, but not.
Chimes resonate to heart.
Anxious – heart tight.
Wall to hang onto
    Vibrating from the inside out.
Heartbeat in my head.
Analyzing.
Bell, visitors coming. Dong.
Tight in my chest
But calm, more sleepy though.
Calming, but possible

Tired now.

Rain is letting up on the glass

windowpanes.

Can't see past. Smeared water,

raindrops wash away the pain,

Still there under the surface

I had to see if the rain is really there.

Gradually getting louder.

In my distant mind.

Now picking up speed.

Intensify

    the rain. Coming down.

I am glad it's almost over.

HANGING ON

Rush of water
Following a path
    A jagged edge.
    Closing in the gaps
Choking
Holding
Sustaining
Ready to come up now.
    How?!
Waiting for a break.
Wind to pass
Rush by my space without a
word.
No sound now.
Gulping for air
Coming up again and again.
Choking
Holding
Sustaining
Peeking through
A glimmer of light = Hope
Hang on.
    That's How.

DISTRACT

Too many distractions!

Not really allowing myself

to open up and feel.

Fidgety --- want to get things done.

Can't concentrate.

The dongs are hurting my ears,

bells are annoying.

Not peaceful or quiet within.

Almost like a racket, with flowing water.

Too much noise within

and outward.

Can't wait until this is over.

Have to be somewhere.

Have to do something.

Pushed for time.

No time to open up

and sit still.

DIS-TRACTIONS

Requires a lot of energy

to just sit still

and go within

No time

    Where to go?

What is important?

Choose your space.

Stay open to the sound

of the vibrations.

You can barely hear them.

Distractions

    Dis – tract – ions

    Disconnected <u>not</u> on

    track, ions!

That damn loud bell again

Clanging like church

Like an assembly

Too loud, too many people

Can't breathe or see

Slow it down.

A train run away on its

tracks – can't stop it now.

Beautiful meadow on the
other side.
Buttercups, lilac, roses,
flowers flowing and
blowing in the wind.

A butterfly lands on my nose.
He is colorful.
Talking with a whisper
rubbing his legs together.

I am here. I am here.
I am here for YOU.
You matter. You are loved.

There is a lot to learn.

PERSISTENT PRESSURES

Energy flowed from side to side.

Still there – a pressure.

Antsy when started.

Now a huge pounding and

pressure at both sides of head

Near ears

Still persists above

Right

Eye

Eyebrow

Ache

Not

Now

CONSTANT PRESSURES

Anxious

Impatient

Sounds annoying

Rain falling too loud

Steady notes held ok,

    satisfying

Bells make me feel hurried

I forgot something

At the end

Relaxed, refreshed

But tired.

Sleepy

My mind feels like a "stuck pillow."

Cloudy inside

    and somewhat noisy.

Always a pressure

Over my

Right

Eye

LIFE

LIFE

Do you ever just wonder why Life is worth it?

LIFE....how is it that it always has to end? Life will end in sorrow.

It WILL END. Why?

The passage of time between two people, distances, worlds.

DEATH

Until death do us part....

I guess that is the truth. The real truth. Death will make us part, it is an ending.

It is a separation from the physical self forever.

Why?

When will it end? No one ever knows. That is the eternal secret.

No one ever escapes it. We think we can with drugs, freedom, fun, and excitement. But with all the "living" in between, it will still end.

So why? Why do we think it is all worth it?

I keep asking myself these questions. I am not sure why.

I guess the smiles on my family members' faces, the wonder, the awe, the telling me "I love you Mommy"…the cuts and bruises, the scrapes….picking them up and holding them close.

But someday even that will end. They will no longer need us. We will then need them. It is the circle of life. It just is.

"Parting is such sweet sorrow." Said Shakespeare. I get it. To depart this world is to take apart everything you know. The wisdom left behind either gets lost or gets taught. Either way it is a death. It always ends in death.

SHATTERED TO PIECES

How many pieces must one break into?

I mean, truly, infinite?

    Until there is nothing left but atoms.

A cell, a muscle, a time in space…all have memory.

    Memories are created with a wholeness, not snips and pieces.

When you get down to only pieces, you are shattered.

    And scattered.

    And scared.

    And ready to drop down to your knees and ask "Why?"

You need to relieve this pressure.

This dichotomy of build-up and release.

All this pain is not good for the soul.

    Split-Soul

Already shattered.

Already scattered about.

Hard to find the millions of pieces.

Ready to burst through like a dam…

    Niagara Falls, gushing, rushing to its depths down below…

    I bet that feels exhilarating.

    A release beyond the depths of my soul.

Hard to imagine such freedom.

The flow of energy of the water is unstoppable.

How does one venture to be like Niagara Falls?

Never-ending,

    always releasing,

        a refreshing sight for your mind and body.

The orbs of light

    caused by the sunshine peeking through.

Even these orbs are dancing and laughing,

    playing with the light before your very eyes.

The water as it hits the bottom,

    connecting to its flow – pieces shattered,

    scatter to the surface,

    rising up so the tourists can feel its moisture.

Atoms of water traveling at a momentous speed.

They migrate, disappear and do not care to "re-unite" with the bigger body of water.

Is it because these smaller atoms do not care?

They are ready to be released from the stronghold of the magnificent waterfall.

Just as you could…

Release those shattered pieces into the spaces
Ask for guidance as parts of your split-soul take a new course.
Perhaps some will return,
      still haunting your mind and spirit,
      still wreaking havoc in your body.

Let the memories through,
      working through each and every one.
Allowing yourself to feel again,
      one step at a time.

Coming up for air in a stifling world.
Taking a stronghold on your mind.

Waiting for that burst of energy,
your own waterfall cascading up and out,
flowing like a light,
millions of shattered, scattered pieces
coming together,
     once again
     to let you know
     you can feel the
     orbs of light
     the moisture on your face
     the expanse surrounding your soul

in a healing energy
only you can create.

Waiting for you to experience
the full spectrum of freedom
the joy, the delight,
        once again.

Air rushing in to your soul, gasping for breath.
Trying to learn to live again.
So you can be released from this chokehold.
So you can feel the exhilaration
And reap the rewards

Split-Soul
        no more
Come together
Unite the scattered pieces,
while releasing some into the ground,
never to be seen again.

Prepare for your own waterfall,
        Cascading through your tears,
Touching each moment,
Orbs of light peeking
        through the shiny, salty feelings

Let these emotions wash out and

come up to the shore.

Breathe again.

Renew,

Become the soul

designed as you.

Refreshing to say the least.

A sense of wonder and enjoyment again.

Let it all creep back in.

Wash away the dirt and hurt.

Let Niagara Falls be your guide.

Its magnificence is true and can see you through.

> In your mind
>
> In your soul
>
> Making you whole.
>
> The essence of your being
>
> ready to stand up again.

Migrating to a new place.

Calibrating the new you.

Figuring out what to do.

Shattered to pieces.

Work it through and through.

Designed to move at immense speeds.

Rushing to make it all happen. So you

can come together

let it out

fill it up

do it again

And find your own steady rhythm of immense flow,

    a continuum

    of your scattered pieces

To find your own path to that

      Waterfall of freedom.

STILLNESS

Be still.

Go against the flow.

Make your emotions stable.

Do not let them wane

and wander.

Go with the smallest

voice from within ---

     Listen to it!

     It is real.

God-driven voice

Growing bigger in your

mind and heart.

Let it be heard.

Act on it.

Follow your destiny.

Choose your own path.

Be still.

Be free.

Do not get caught up in
the tidal wave.

Emotions come and go.
Your voice doesn't.
Let it exist.
Let it heal you.

Your body has knowledge.
Respect it.
Purity.
Strength.
Love.

Conquer your fears.

SCREAMIN' FROM THE INSIDE

A stifled cry
Trying to make its way out.

Never to be heard or seen.
Who is to care?

The pain runs deep.
    Too deep.
Why does it happen?

This journey of pain is
overwhelming.
Needing a place to stay
Needing a way to get out.

A low lengthy scream
Can't be heard.
Quieted on the inside by
the constricted muscles of
my throat.

God where is my strength
to believe?!
Can't you hear me
Screamin' on the inside?

A damn bursts and still
I can't be heard.
I thought my spirit
was strong, but it
is stretched thin.

Why can't justice prevail?
Is it that difficult
to see the truth?!

This is why the scream
cannot be heard ---
no one believes the
truth. No one cares.
Life moves on and you
are left behind.

Belief, justice, honesty,
Simple concepts.

Filled with a whole lot of hope.

Hope slashed in half and then

in half again, 'till there's

not even a glimmer left.

Sitting in the darkness.

Not heard.

Not seen.

Empty

Except for a stifled

scream.

TAPPING

TAPPING

Tunnel

Activates

Pace

Poses

Invites

Negativity

Greatness

BOXES OF YOUR SOUL

Your soul
    compartmentalized
in little boxes
Waiting to be freed
from the inner confines
of your mind.
Light emitting from
the edges of the boxes.
Peeking ever so
Gracefully around
and through
each crevice.
Light emanates
from your soul
When you are happy.
Light guides you to
greater places
than you can climb alone.
Darkness keeps you
in these boxes.
Away from light.

Away from the

essence of your soul.

Grab on to the first

rung of the ladder

and climb.

Soar to the top...

<u>You</u> be the eagle that

looks out and up into the light.

Keep going.

Your inner flame

will not burn out.

Watch it grow and

learn. Go forth and tell the

world who <u>you</u> really are.

You are special.

You are worth it.

You are Light.

Come out of the darkness and show

your true self.

Do not be afraid.

I will guide you.

I will provide the small steps

to a bigger, more fulfilling life

Trust in me.

My God.

    My Light.

    My new brightness

    shines forth.

    Thank you.

SPLIT-SOLE

Split-sole

Pieces of your soul split open

and scatter about

Just like the rhythm of your soles

hitting the ground

It is difficult to sew them back in

The rough spots smooth over in time

only to be gouged back open over

and over again.

FEAR

FEAR: **F**ace **E**verything **A**bove your **R**each

What is it really?

A Fear of dying?

A Fear of not being in control?

A Fear of not being loved?

A Fear of no connection?

A Fear of not participating in life?

A Fear of missing out?

I don't know. But I know Fear is controlling. It is real. It is inside and outside. It is everywhere. It permeates your soul. It clogs your mind. It chooses for you. It cannot be good for you.

What is Freedom?

Freedom to choose your own path. A way to your happiness. A way to climb out. A way to breathe and feel. A way to realize dreams again. A way to experience life to the fullest. A way to imagine. A way to live and learn. A way to new challenges.

Which will you choose?

Or will you let fear choose for you?

PUT GOD FIRST?

Put God First?

How do you find so much faith?

How do you put it first when your beliefs are always challenged?

What do you say when your own dreams are shattered?

Or when you don't truly believe that dreams can come true to ordinary people?

How is it possible?

Do you put God First?

IF WALLS COULD TALK

If walls could talk

if walls could talk they would remember the most beautiful memories the family is making

if walls could talk they would light up from the inside out and smile with remembrance of each and every person living inside its walls

if walls could talk they would have clouds inside their walls to capture the sorrow and sadness and the pain so that it can float up to the heavens and disappear and all negativity would be erased from living within its walls…if walls could talk.

CYPRESS

Cypress

Tried-and-true

stand tall like a cactus

cut into Woodside

scarred for life

but still strong.

Overbearing

powerful

elegant

yet simple

requiring nothing

standing tall

providing

Giving

Trees

PANIC

When in panic ---
    feelings of

unknown

stuck

smooshed in line

no air left

can't go back where

    I got in --- line closed up of people

    opening closes behind me

    have to look ahead

    and not behind.

Head split on right side,

then come together.

Not a headache.

Like a "rearranging."

Spinning.

Closing-in feeling.

Air not moving. Swirling around, stagnant air.

    Will there be enough air for everyone to breathe?

Being on fire.

Do not get stuck in it.

> Going down stairs, very crowded.

> Can't breathe.

> Don't want to get lost.

> Running down stairs on the right hand side.

> On the outskirts.

Wait for me.

Need a distraction.

Can't talk a lot.

Brain going constantly, lots of energy - - - so hard to focus.

Tiring.

> Panic attacks again.

UNDERSTANDING THE SHADOWS

Remove yourself.

Uproot yourself.

Pull yourself up.

    Up out of the shadows.

    Up and out.

    Up and out.

Come to the surface.

Don't dip down.

Break through.

Do what you can.

Accept yourself.

Break through.

A rough patch

    Hit it hard.

    Come. Go through it.

    With me.

Make light of the shadows.

SENSE OF SURROUNDINGS

Bump.

The in-out whoosh of your breath.

Melodic bells chiming.

A simple melody. Catchy.

Do you want to hum?

A car whizzes by. Stops. No sound.

Ding.

Pound. Pound. Hammering

Still that ever-present slightly

high-pitched sound of a bell

slowly swaying in the breeze.

Light catches your eyelids.

Close them to feel the sunshine on the inside.

A child's voice. Can't make it out.

A dog's tags jingling as he moves easily through the garden.

The orange blossoms smell along with the fresh scent of lemons.

The quick-witted hummingbird making its way from flower to flower.

You can barely make out its wings from the constant fluttering.

The gentle breeze talking to you, bumping your arm.

Beckoning you to take another breath.

In-out whoosh of your breath.

Filling your lungs with fresh fuel for the day.

Close your eyes to see the pink haze on your eyelids.

Did God create that color?

Look up!

An endless sky. Treating you to a whole new world.

Traveling to a more expansive place.

Away from the sorrow and the heartache of the here and now.

You can escape the boredom, the tears, the monotony of this place.

Look around.

Light glistens through the empty spaces of the leaves on the trees.

Barely moving or making a sound.

The chimes gently talk to each other.

Ding. Ding.

    Dong.

A bouncy conversation.

No words allowed.

Swirling, flowing water of a brook nearby

Constantly in motion. Crouch down to touch it.

Interrupting its flow for only an instant.

It goes back and picks up the pace.

A whippoorwill.

    Who-who-whooo-whooo.

What is he chirping?

Cars whiz by again.

Jingling tags of a beloved pet.

Still the sunshine flows through your skin.

You can escape...

    If you close your eyes

    And just listen.

The sounds of nature will catapult you away

to where your soul will find its message.

Don't be afraid to go there.

For just an instant of peace.

You will find joy in the beauty of nature's silence.

The in-out whoosh of your breath.

It becomes magical.

It becomes a vehicle to take you there.

You never know where you might land.

Trust it. Breathe in Breathe out.

The wind will nudge you if you go too far.

You will be transported back.

Just open your eyes.

The pink haze will disappear.

The bright sun will be great.

And you can return to your imaginary land anytime.

> For an instant, an hour, time and time again.

FREEDOM TO BE

What can happen when you go inside your mind and heart?

Can you hear it? The low strumming of a sound so faint that even your heart can't bear it.

Why is it necessary to go there?

Others simply cannot understand this message if they have not experienced it first.

And why would they even want to go there?

No, it is yours and yours alone.

A burden so heavy, it is hard to shed and peel those layers off.

Could money buy the Freedom To Be? Could money be the only way out to hide behind this shame?

Money buys Freedom, not love.

We create our own love.

Money buys time, so you can focus on things you love and care about.

But could money be the Freedom you need to get out of your head?

Does it help you buy the justice you need in our broken system?

It could.

But so could honesty. And it is free.

Honesty may not get you there completely. But at least you have the face that is willing to look in the mirror at yourself, although broken and incomplete, to know you have the Freedom To Be.

There may be others along the path that deter your way.

It is ok.

It is ok to choose something different.

It is ok to choose your own broken path. Who knows?
This path may lead you to a better life of Freedom To Be.

Sometimes when we look inside our mind and heart, they are in opposition.

Your heart is feeling the burden, the truth, the unfurling of the colors that once were so vivid.

Your mind is nagging at the ones who don't believe you, trying to get them to simply understand.

This creates confusion. This creates dissonance. This creates a sound so low that the humming is faint and almost unreal.

But you know, you truly know, that this sound is the way your heart beats when it is mourning your losses. Only you know the constant humming is the faint sounds of your heart trying to survive. Trying to live in a world and trying to find its own path to its Freedom To Be.

Perhaps we all should look inside that deep pocket of time and try to read our own heart and mind.

It is ok to go there.

It is ok to go deeply.

It is ok to feel.

And it is ok to finally breathe and let go and

Be The Freedom.

LESSONS

Whatever the case, it is drowning me…

 Please help me God, what is next?

I can't feel it.

I can't figure it out.

I can't move ahead.

I don't know how.

 How to move, ahead, behind, beside, or through. How to breathe again and simply let my body do its job.

I am simply stuck.

 Stuck in this immoveable world. No air swirling around my face.

 My lungs getting smaller without any air. Unable to breathe. Unable to get in just a dash of hope and light and peace.

How to go forward.

 Do I simply turn around? Do I choose the right or the left? Do I stay put? Or do I make my own new path instead of the already-trodden one?

Leave the past as lessons.

 What lessons? Had enough. Still drowning. Can't hold on to nothing.

How are others so fearless?

 Maybe they hide it, unlike me.

Maybe they too are drowning, in a downward spiral of depression and sadness and trauma…trying to find their way out of the maze of emotions.

Maybe they too are not aware of the lessons yet and feel cheated.

Maybe they too are constantly stuck in their head, unable to move.

Unable to feel.

Unable to simply turn their head.

Unable to breathe a new breath of fresh air.

Feeling stuck. No way out.

Perhaps hiding it behind their many walls of concrete.

Packing it away in little compartments too solid to pry open anymore.

We need to help each other learn these lessons.

Yes, I know these lessons are unique.

I know each one of us has our own to learn.

But why can't we be helped along the way?

A little prodding,

A little encouragement,

Just a smile,

A hug,

A sense of kinship,

A way to connect in
this lonely
immoveable world.

We can be a pillar of support for the zombie next to us.

We can be that smile on the outside,

so that the inside

will match up

with that slight glimmer of hope

and love

and peace

on your fellow human being's face.

Then that zombie will slowly,

slowly,

ever so slowly

melt away into a new form,

A new shape,

A new being with a renewed sense of spirit.

A spirit so strong it can be felt across the
miles,

across the deserts,

across all the hatred and fears and
loneliness.

Lessons learned….wisdom and truth and love and peace.

BALANCED FROM THE INSIDE

A strong connection

    seen yet not.

Held together by an invisible string.

A constant flow of energy

    bubbling up from the inside.

Trying to stay light and balanced.

Keeping the mind out of the mix.

Don't let the dark thoughts enter the space.

Gently swaying, swirling, coming to the surface

    of your aura,

Yet not letting go

    of the stability inside,

Hiding, but confident in its constant flowing connection

      to your inner peace.

Struggle no longer

Find harmony within.

Make it easy for yourself

And find your own

balance of energy inside.

Bring forth your lightness,

    your aura, so it can shine through

        Your colors are so bright.

        Let them sparkle and shine ---

           without a thought of holding back.

Memories are painful, like toxic waste.

Let the old self shed off,

    a shadow left in the dark and

    the toxins will slowly disappear.

This balance from the inside

    will recalibrate

    and find your new self.

Don't forget to explore.

You will find it.

Be free in flight.

But enjoy the process.

Heal in your own light.

Find it and let go.

Renew again and again and again.

    You are...

Balanced From The Inside.

LINES

Clean Lines

    II

    II

Shows a set path

    II

    II

    I_____

        _____Does it lead to truth or darkness?

            I I

            I I

             I I

_____I I

_____I

    II

Come along for this journey.

    II_____And_____

        II

        Create your own lines.

They don't have to be "clean."

For you are clean and whole inside.

The outside is simply a
  refraction of light,
  playing with your mind.

Think like this.

Your soul is whole.

Your spirit may break in pieces,
  tattered and torn,
    but it mends with ridges, valleys,
   twists and turns.
These imperfect lines
  are clean.
They are truth.
They tell a story from beginning
         to middle
          to end.

Your soul knows the way.

Continue to listen to the path.
Your path is wide open.
Only you can fill those ridges.

Keep them in your soul, but

    don't forget to give.

        Faith

        Love

        Hope

        Serenity

        Purpose.

Your purpose can be found

    as you fill in and

    mend the cracks and

    close the doors to the past, and

    jump out the windows of your soul

    into the future.

Your lines will support you.

    II

Your squiggles and

    twists and

        turns and

            ruts and

                crevices will continue to

                    nourish your
                    soul.

You just have to be brave enough

to keep filling in the gaps.

The gaps fulfilled

become your life.

Your purpose.

Your whole soul.

Your complete circle

of wavy, curvy lines.

These lines will sustain you

from the

Beginning through

the Middle and

all the Way to

The End.

MINDFULNESS

Mindfulness

Mind you.

Mind me.

    Mend us.

    We three.

THE ROOT

Our Root starts our

    Growth.

Growth starts our

    Evolution.

Evolving every day

    begins our journey.

    of healing.

    of mindfulness.

    of being present.

    of contentment.

    of peace.

Being oneself, all the parts within start to heal.

The outer shell begins to die off.

The dragons will be slayed.

The pieces inside

    start to grow together again.

Melding into a more

    understanding, empathetic and

    whole You.

You cannot continue to compartmentalize your experiences.

All of our experiences create our whole self.

What if you just cut out the negative aspects of yourself?

    Why do that?

    You would no longer be whole.

    You would be a portion.

    A portion unserved.

If you keep the negatives hidden,

    You will never find peace.

For it is in growth, you will evolve and learn.

And it is in learning, that you will start to become

    whole again.

If you quiet your madness,

    What is left?

    A hole.

    An empty space.

    With no air to buoy it.

But…

If you combine the growth of your soul with the

    bad and good experiences,

      you will start to fill those empty spaces with air ---

        becoming one with love, light and peace.

This is the <u>ROOT</u> <u>ALL</u> <u>TOLD</u>.

PONDERING

Fears creeping up.

    Assess the situation.

Inside your air is compressed.

    No longer a way out.

What is this fluttering of

Fearful emotion?

Who causes it?

Why is it there?

How do I crack the code?

Adventure is unknown.

To be curious is to advance

Why then is the unknown so fearful?

    Is it death?

    Will I get hurt?

    Will I lose my family?

Inside it is swirling around.

Will I lose my ability to decipher a way out?

Will there be others to care?

    Who will help?

Do I plow right through anyway?

Do I try it in spite of my fears?

What is right or wrong?

No one can tell me.

But my head needs to shut up and listen.

Fears creeping in.

LET GO OF YOUR FEARS

Let Go of Your Fears
Faces, finding someone that cares
Will you hear me? Will you truly be there?

On a branch, climbing high. Don't look down. You won't drown.
Onward you climb. Keep grounded. Stay still. Catch up your
mind.
Suddenly, another branch, a simple twig. Will it bend? Will it
break?
Take it and run. Run high and low. Nowhere else to go. Up, up,
up.

Try something new. Clear your mind. Cleanse your soul.

Maybe your inner dance will start to move again. Slowly at first,
then it will spin, then it will soar. Coax it out of its shell. Try to
break new ground.
Again, try again, and again. You will fall a bit, but you will not
stay here. You will not be stuck. There is a glimmer of hope,
somewhere inside of you, just waiting like a pearl to shine again
and be new.

Take it and go. Go here and there. Nowhere else but here. Go
far. Stray from the path.
It will bend. It will not break. You will not get lost.
There is a new light to guide you. It will lead you to a new peace.
An inner sight will guide you there.

Try something new. Clear your mind. Cleanse your soul.

Maybe your heart will open a little. Chisel away at the darkness and slowly light will find its way through the cracks. You will find love again. Passions will ignite.
Scratch the surface, find the twig and use it. Pry it open and find the pearl. The blackness will subside. Swirling colors will take its place. You will learn to see again. You can see your inner mind. It is there. It is alive. You are well.
You are healing.

See the world now through a new lens. Everything is new again. Be still. Onward you climb.
Keep grounded. Keep your energy swirling. Will you dare?

Faces, turn around.
There is a face that cares.
Someone will hear you.
Someone will see you.
Someone will love you.
You will heal and when you do, you will be that face that turns around for another.
You are the branch. Be the connection.
Let Go of Your Fears.

POINT UNKNOWN

Point Unknown
  Like a pencil
    One does not know where it lands on the paper
Point Unknown
  Like a compass
    One does not know where it twirls
Point Unknown
    Like the waves of the ocean
    One does not know where they start or end
Point Unknown
    Like a coin thrown up in the sky
      One does not know where it will land on the ground and
      which side will show
Point Unknown
    Like a song on the piano
      One does not know where the chords and melody will lead
      you
Point Unknown
    Like your emotions
      One does not know how long they will last nor what to do
      about them
Point Unknown
    Like a bird in flight
      One does not know where her wings will bring her or if
      she will continue to soar
Point Unknown
    Like a place on the map
      One does not know if it truly exists

Point Unknown
    Like the wind and the breezes
        One does not know in which direction to turn
Point Unknown
    Like your mind making a decision
        One does not know.

P.T.S.D.

P.T.S.D.

Post
  Traumatic
    Stress
      Disorder
  P.T.S.D.
       Pay
       To
       Sit
       Down
  P.T.S.D
     Pry
       Try
         See
           Do
P.T.S.D.
  Plug
  Tamp
  Surrender
  Dig
P.T.S.D.
     Partly
       Together
            Separated
                  Detached

P.T.S.D.
Pull it together
Try to pray it out
Smile and move on
Ditch it and do it again.

P.T.S.D.
A surrender, a halting.
No one knows why or how.
Every one is different.
Quietly suffocating in your thoughts.
Don't know what to do.
Thinking is scattered yet constant.
    Snippets here and there
Trying not to remember.
    Nightmares. Blank stares.
Stuffing it all inside. Tamp it down tight. Plug it up forever. Do
not dig it up.
Surrender. STOP. PTSD. STOP.
No need to return there.
Please listen.

P.T.S.D.
    Partly Together. (stand tall)
    Separated. (no one hears you)
      Detached. (mind, body and soul ripped apart)
P.T.S.D.
No one knows. It does not show. The outside is rigid.
The inside is scared, anxious, broken, defeated.
Fluttering, dizzying, spinning
Swirling to a new you.
Breaking the tether.
Until you break free.
      But when? And how many times until you land?

Plug
Tamp
Surrender
Dig
> Plug it up.
> Tamp it down.
> Surrender and release.
> Dig it out. Again and again and again.
>> Until you scar over again.
>> And start the healing process again.
>> Ready to dig it out. A new layer this time.
>> Another surrender and release.

Surrender and release
Release
Release
Release
Release. Renew. Regrow. Regain. Repair. Release.
> Again and again.

P.T.S.D.   Until the next time. Again.

P.T.S.D.   Pay To Sit Down. Be your own voice. Listen to
yourself.

P.T.S.D.   Push To Stay Deep. Because within the deep, you will
find solitude, you will find solace, you will find answers, you will
learn to piece your soul together with string, tape, cement,
whatever it takes. Whatever you need to heal. It is your surrender,
your halting. Each is their own. No one knows why or how. No
need to suffocate yourself any longer. No need to barely survive.
Come out of the darkness. There is light.
Renew. Regrow. Regain. Repair. Release.
Little by little. Again and again. Every step matters.
P.T.S.D. **P**ut **T**ogether **S**erious **D**etours. **STOP. PTSD.**

THROUGH THE PURPLE HAZE

Through the Purple Haze
   A layer deep within the recesses of your soul
Gather up your strength to learn anew
     Perhaps a yellow streak, or an orange bolt, a continuous line
     White sparks, coming at you to catch
The Purple Haze becomes brighter and more defined.
   You are within that protection.
   Light feeling with heavy surroundings. Moving
   soundlessly.
   Invisible to the dangers ahead.
Through the Purple Haze.
   Marching along, hoping to conquer your thoughts.
One step, one breath at a time.
One sound. It carries over to the next.
What lies ahead?
   Quietly you peek.
What are you trying to get to?
 What are you trying to reach?
    Is it your spirit leading you through the Purple Haze?
     Trying to get you to hear?
    To see?
     To touch?
      To feel again?
   To taste the kindness that still exists.
   To tell you it is ok. Ok to proceed ahead. Ok to move
   beyond your fears.
Go gently through the Purple Haze.
But do go through it.
Through the Purple Haze.
   A layer deep within the recesses of your soul.

Trying to teach you to hear, to see, to touch, to feel.
It is ok. It is real. Feel it surround your being.

Use it as a blanket, a shield of protection, without the brick walls.

Use it to catch the guiding yellow streak, the orange bolt, the jagged edges, the continuous lines, the sparks coming at you one at a time. Catch them all.

Find a way...
Through the Purple Haze.

SHORT CIRCUIT

Upended again.
Ripped through the heart and soul.
Don't know which way to go.

Retreat slowly...until only the tip of your nose shows.
Like a wolf in hiding.
Nothing flows.
Striding and sliding.

Coming forward.
Only to come out short circuited.
No one cares. You are there to reveal the truth.
Court circuit.
Short circuit.

They only want to pull the plug and short circuit you.
You mustn't let them.
Reveal the truth, don't conceal it.
The ball keeps rolling and the mountain is treacherous.
Like a stew, you are through.

Friends will disappear. Like a leper, you seem to them.
Shine through this storm.
Plucked like a stem.
This is NOT the norm.

There is room for you in here.
Come and share this crowded space.
With so many others over there.
Going at a snail's pace.

When will the jeers stop?
Stares pop.
Jabs at beliefs.
What a thief!

Constant scrutiny.
This is mutiny.

Then angels appear out of nowhere.
Soothe your fears.
Help the stares subside.

Encourages the truth to come out.
Stays on your side.
Finds a new path for you.
Sends light and flickering flames to let you know "this too shall pass."
Can candlelight talk?
You might want to take a walk.

Moonlight shines.
Finds you alone in your thoughts.
Trying to just breathe.
Not to get caught.

Resting but barely.
Quickly pick up the pace.
Don't want to see his face.
Surely it will fade in time.
Will these memories be mine?

Short circuit.
Court circuit.
Pulled the plug again.
When will it end?
Wire breaks in half.
On the mend.
   Again and again.

Truth will reveal itself once more.
Angels show up at your door.
Tell you to live and smile.
Try to stay awhile.

Short circuit.
Unjustly revealed.
Maybe you should appeal?
It is NOT fair. No one cares.
Upended again. Is it just a game to them?
Caught in a snare.
He is triumphant again.
You can't turn around. Not a sound.
Maybe the Angels lied.
No, they are by my side.

Show me the way.
There is no time to play.
Just please stay.
Angels are triumphant.
Seemingly insignificant.
Yet trumpets continue to play.
Sounds in the distance to be heard.
They will return. Your truth will be heard.
Never to be short circuited anymore.

THROUGH THE PORTICO

Through The Portico
Clear blue sky and white cotton swirls
Gently swaying, each and every leaf
One point reaching to the next
Every little twig and branch
Hundreds of spectacular points
Light squeezing through the portico
Sturdy and still
Winding up and around the spaces
Letting in the air and gentle breezes
Transversing through the sky
Swirling up into the universe
Rounding up the energy through the portico
Holding its own space
Ready for another encounter
On another lazy day.

SUFFOCATING IN THE DARKNESS

Take a deep breath. Let it go all the way in.
Keep up the rhythm.
Slow it down now, in and out, just breathe
Flowing, flowing, you should not have to think about it.

A pinch, a chokehold, coming around.
Starting to close off
Pulse getting faster, can't get out
Pressure, gripping, closing

No more strength
Starting to fade
Coming up for air
Darkness sets in, enveloping you in fear
Suffocating in the darkness

You have to breathe, you have to count.
Sneak in a breath, a wiggle of air
Rising to the surface, going in
Will it reach my lungs?
Will anyone care?

Pushing you down deeper
To a level past breath
A calm reserve of nothingness
Just be, nothing to think about
You can't

Return to the surface again,
Trying, trying to see on the outside
Get rid of this suffocation on the inside
Enveloping you in a deep abyss

Perhaps it is worthless
Not worth the fight
There will only be remnants
And the pieces cannot be sewn together
Random thoughts continue coming up

Struggle through the darkness
It is only a color
It is not happening again

Let the breath continue
Pulse slows, fears subsides

Take control of the darkness
The suffocating is no more
You are in a new place
It is ok, to be safe, and breathe again.

When it returns, it will be easier
You are not meant to stay there in the dark
Turn your breath to the sky
Take it all in, just try
Meandering thoughts again...

How many times will it return?
Create a new space
Turn it around in your mind,
Clean the air around you
Ask for protection

Now, when the dusk is starting,
Go to a place of resilience
And fight. Do not fly away
Send in your angels, guided by your thoughts
Settling in to a new space
One that envelops you in love, not fear

Making the suffocation a distant memory
Not to be forgotten, but to be marked
By growth and time and healing
Hanging on to a new day dawning
Waiting for the new colors to show their face
Creating a web of magic like no other

Guiding you to a place of mystery
Without the fear
Without the doubt
Without the hesitation
Wanting to move ahead
Through the maze of life...
    in a new wonderous way

Forging a new memory not to be forgotten
Making your mark
Creating a whirlwind of color
Showing up, knowing it matters
For the next ones to learn
And hoping beyond hope that no one...
    Suffocates in the dark again.

THE EYES OF A CHILD

Seemingly insignificant
As you watch them go back and forth
They are telling you a message
If you would just listen
Never mind what you think
Just listen to how you feel

Hear the child's truth.
See the child's fear.
Continue to listen.
You will be amazed how much they know.
In a room full of strangers, that child knows.

The eyes of a child
They say so much
There is no need for idle chatter
See the hurt and the pain
Help this child
It could be the best decision you've made

Bring that child a blanket
Warm their fears of tomorrow
Reach their heart with warmth
Smile upon their soul
Grieve beside them, but bring them up again
Hug them tight, for tomorrow may not come

Know that you did the right thing
Climbing into their space
See the eyes of a child

Hear the hurt and pain
Touch all their todays
Listen to what they need
And bring the hope of tomorrows
Back to their heart again.

TRUST

Dedicated to Sue K. for our mutual trust and respect, and for teaching me that trust and respect must be <u>earned</u>, not given.

Trust
Keep it real
Out in the open
Five letters to show you care
Trust
Be a friend
Do not bend
You will never regret it
Trust
But if you don't
You will see
What you did to me
Trust
It may not earn
You any stars
But you will be yourself
Trust
In the mirror
Only time will tell
If you truly did
Trust
If you show
Your true side
You will be rewarded
Trust
Not by anyone
But who cares
If you have to live with you

Trust
Continue to tell
The whole story
Even if no one cares
Trust
Someday
Someone will come along
And you will be heard
Trust
Hold your head high
Keep it steady
For you will not be stopped
Trust
In a nutshell
It is not hard
Say what's on your mind
Trust
But if you sway
They will know
And you will not be forgiven
Trust
Hard to to do
In times of trouble
Despair or sorrow
Trust
It will show
Through the muck
And give you strength to grow
Trust
If you break it
It can't be mended
At least not without hesitation
Trust
So if you can
Give it all you got
And make it right
Trust.

A CRIPPLING MOMENTUM

Rippling through the waves
Rhythmic pulsing like a song never-ending
Joyously jumping ever so lightly
Speeding up, slowing down, halt, dead stop
Crippling your momentum.

Short bursts of fire
Up and down, going higher
Put out the light
Down, forever out, dead stop
Crippling your momentum.

Air waves carry your voice
Thin air, thick air, heavy with sound
Carrying on from one breath to the next
Catch it in mid-air
Smothered, smushed, silent, dead stop
Crippling your momentum.

Soft and cushiony
Buoyant and bouncy
Comfortable and worn
Telling you to just hold on
Letting go, dead stop
Crippling your momentum.

Dead
Stop
Crippling your momentum
Not your moment
Return to the inside.

Don't let it die
Find the light that shines
Pick it up and check it out
Haltingly, slowly, going forward

See how many steps you can take
Rough patches will smooth out
Go around the bend and peek a little farther
   It only takes a moment
   To pick up your momentum
   And reach monstrous heights
To turn the crippling momentum
Into a cavernous hole to whence it came
And continue your movement
On a path to freedom and peace

THE TIME HAS COME

The time has come to stop and listen
Gather around
Say not a sound

You will learn
What you need through prayer
No one cares
Just sit and stare

Gather around the fire-pit
Just sit and sit
And see what you get

Motionless
Speechless
Less and less
Breathless

Turn around
Don't make a sound
Just pick it up
And see what you've found

Stare at it awhile
Even if it's not your style
Put it in the pile
And think about the miles

Return to the present
Hope you made a dent
Angels were sent
Gifts were only leant
So you could see what they meant.

Pass it on and then...
When the time has come to stop and listen
Gather around
Say not a sound
Don't ask when
That was then...
The time has come
Let's have some fun!

WIRED SHUT

Almost ready, hold it steady
Crazy space
Out of place

Don't despair
I know it's not fair
They want you to get caught in the lair

Find a way out
Seek it now
Before you fall
And lose your gall

The nerve of it all
Wired shut
Don't get cut
Make a path and stall

In between
Find it floating
They will see you gloating

What they don't know
You will show
Find it hard no more
And come upon the shore.

Almost ready, hold it steady
Crazy space
Out of place no more.

IF ONLY

Dedicated to my Dad

If only there were more time
    To do the things you want to do
If only there was an ocean
    In which the kids can play and frolic
If only you could take the sand with you
    In a bottle to transport you to another time
If only
    There would be another breath to hold onto
If only
    Then the light would shine all around
If only everyone's dreams would come true
If only
    Then there would be sparks in their eyes
    Not sorrow and pain
If only
    Then grief would be diminished
If only a tear could bring joy again
    Then all would not be lost
      Then change would be seen as a welcome transformation
      Not another world you wish to escape
If only
    Perhaps you could decide
    If only you knew how

THE WALK

Sliver of Blue
Powdery soft and true
Red White and Blue
Sing praises to you

A ray of light
Shining down
And all around
Capturing the ground

Soul of White
Shines so bright
Angels sing in the night
And will return in might

Rainbows of Red
Seem to delight
Pick up the rhythm
Who said happiness is dead?

Leaves scatter about
Barely touching the surface
A soft crinkling in the wind
Footsteps find...

    Soft, trodden pathways
    A bit of mulch,
    Pine needles nestling,
    Petals moist with dew
    Perhaps a fairy or two?

Safe in the forest
Clear the chatter in your head
Look around and forge your path upon the ground
Stop and rest, go ahead

Mushroom tea parties
An animal's delight
Take flight
And see the light

Reach the edge, around the bend
'Till you can see no more
Another path leads you to
White oak and owls to send

Stones alight in every which way
Some with lichen, some with dew
Tumbling out to reach you
Telling you not to stew

A quavering creek
Bubbling with joy
Curving and twisting with desire
Growing bigger until it bursts

Opening its flow into something new
Connecting once again with the land
Waterfall flowing and ever growing
Tumultuous sounds abound

Chaos is gone, only nature prevails
Red, White and Blue
Talking to you
Never to let you fall back in the sand

Be brave and stand
Give your senses a bath
Wash all your sorrows away
Find a way to simply stay

Come again on this walk
And we will continue to talk
Taking turns on the way
Sliver of Blue, Soul of White, Rainbows of Red
Your head will feel light
And I promise you only this day.

EMOTIONS ABOUND

All bawled up, sits stuck in my throat
Nowhere to go
Pressure caving in
No choices, no air, something heavy on my head.
Mounting fear, lest there be no air to breathe
A conundrum of panic
Letting loose on all sides
Leading you to a dark tunnel, narrowing, narrowing ever smaller
Nowhere to go
Can't possibly see the other side.
Small spaces, need to expand.
Just get out in time before there is no time
Small stairways leading to doom
Underground tunnels, not a good sight
Sends shivers and makes one's breath freeze in mid-sentence
Lungs crushing, can't seem to breathe
No light at the end of the tunnel
Too many people, too big a crowd
Just a pebble in the middle of the sea
Must get out
Nowhere to go
How does one choose?
Stuck in a panic of fright
Can't turn around, moving ahead like an ant
Heart is pounding, sweat is pouring
The connection to life is lost

Simple kind words, a smile, a nod
Can bring you back to the moment
Look ahead, not down, and right here and now

A bright shining moment is coming
Let me in, beside you, somewhere to go
Ahead, behind, up and down
Choices abound if only you dream them
That get you out of this mess
Crawl out of this space, be free
And connect to the world once again

Slowly, the shaking subsides
The quivers that dance rear up once again
Whilst your mind judges time like a snail
Fear rises and falls
Shutting every door
Needing to retreat to your den

Calmer now, everything sinks in
A sense of peace presides
Flutters still and shakes halt
A thin veil of silence creeps in
Breath becomes deeper and rhythmic again
Ready to pounce on the fright
Keep it steady, you are ready
To face your fears once more.

MESSAGES OF LOVE

Messages
A little tick of the clock
A winding staircase that creaks, leading you up
Sunlight glinting in your hair
Turn around to hear the waves crashing on the rocks
See the little sea lions lounging in the sun
A rainbow peeks through the clouds, wanting to lift up your spirits
A forest path filled with mulch and pine, the smell so enticing it
leads you to take notice of nature
A babbling brook along the way walking alongside of you
Birds chirping their morning song to entice you on your way
A luscious piece of fruit growing from the vine, ready to nourish
you
A gentle breeze to bring you calm

Take notice. This is love.
Messages of love...talking to you.

A beautiful flower floats in your way telling you to start your day
A tiny lizard walks in your path on its way to eat
Your dog nudges you to take a walk and explore
Beautiful mountains standing tall forcing you to look up and out
Over the expansive fields of grass and crops, gently swaying in the
breeze
Over here, saguaro cacti touch the sky
Prickly pear ready to give you nourishing honey and tea
Bright red flowers blooming from its prickly cactus
A moment of peace and calm.

Take notice. This is love.
Messages of love...talking to you.

Bisons roaming the hills, free to be.
The land so expansive the eye cannot take it all in.
Mountains carved by old ancestors.
Pay attention. You may learn something.
A waterfall tucked into the slope of the mountain.
Wonder how it got there?
A winding drive to get you there.
Creates a newness, a oneness with something bigger than you.

Take notice. This is love.
Messages of love...talking to you.

Messages
What can you learn from all this?
Open your senses, see, touch, feel, smell, taste
Expand your mind, open your heart
Pay attention to what is there
Don't fear what isn't
Start your own path to freedom.
Find a way to take notice.
Just breathe and see the messages of love.
Talking to you. Edging you forward. Whispering thoughts.
Find your own connection. You are worth it.

Messages of love...talking to you.

LOST MOMENTS

Lost at sea
Do you need me?
Swimming uphill
What a thrill
Until you stop and drop
Lost in the moment

Poised to climb
What a find
Through the air
I don't care
Lost in the moment

Down below
Tunnel in, darkness surrounds
Care to join?
Pinpoint of light
Through the night
Lost in the moonlight

Feeling fresh
Tramp through the grass
Sunlight reveals
A stretch of time
What will I find?
Lost in the fields

Moments of time
They get away
All day wasted
Minutes not caring
To go back and design
Return to the now
Lost at the moment

Try again
Lift your head
See your spaces
Moments of calm
How do I find?
Friends to share them
Lost in the minute

A bigger picture
There must be more
Hours drive by
How do I share it?
Lost in time

Reveal the past
Trudge right through
Only you
Know the trials
Sit in thought
Return to now
Lost Moments

RACE FOR TIME

Race for time
Get up and go, everything is a race for time
You never finish, you can't start
Try it again and again
Why bother? It ends in a dead end, literally.

So what is the rush?
You can't fit it all in.
Swirling above oneself in a light of green
Need a few moments to let it soak in
Then it just comes up in a rush
Another race for time.

Get it all out, the emotions collide with the race for time
You cannot replace, you cannot dig out
All the junk that rots there waiting for time to heal it
So you smooth it over once again to let it scab over
  Race for time
It is in there,
    waiting for a break in the ice,
    the hidden walls,
    the fortress built
It is too late.
You cannot come in.
The walls are built for strength and protection.

Return to the slab. Try to chisel it out.
Again.
And again,
And yet again.

You are not sure it is worth the wait.
So you close down the gate, seal up the walls and hope there is no
leak.
Until another breakthrough makes you take note
Another race for time.

Is it worth all the hype?
Do you love at first sight?
Do your senses take over again?
Until the love subsides, the spirit dies, and you cannot wait to close
the gate.
Race for time

Keep it moving forward (they say)
Stay in the moment (they say)
Don't look back, the past will hold you there
Don't plan too far ahead (they say)
Or you will miss those present moments (they say)
So why bother with the race for time if we only have to focus on
the now?

It's ok to be late
And not sit at the gate
Look for your own soul's pathway
Of course it's ok to stay and play
But remember to lock down the memories
Yet another race for time

How to proceed, to do any deeds
You cannot even come up for air
One look to the right and one look to the left
Leaves you hanging somewhere in mid-air
Full speed ahead, finish the race

So time won't have time to catch up
But if you look back, it will give you a buck
A jolt so hard you can't move
    And if you remember you stay stuck there
    So that you can't even move
    Stay frozen to the spot?
        I should hope not.
Chisel it out once again.

One foot straight ahead, the other coming quick
Before they can tell you to stop
Weave a bit over there, and a wobble over here
Until you can stand up again

Move forward in time
Go through every step
Never thinking what you may endure
Perhaps you will find that your wall is too tall
And your mind is so full of fear

My dear friend
Once again
It is ok to feel
Come around the fortress and see
    There are others that are waiting
    To be taught what you fear
    Helping you soar off the ground

Take note of the brave
Save goodness instead
Each opportunity abounds
        If you stand up tall
        And stop being small
        Because you weren't meant to live in the ground.

Live on this earth
Before you return to the dirt
To see what you can be
        Take it all in
        Breathe out the sin
        And experience all there is
Never mind what others do
Or think about you
Just piece together a plan
        Do your best
        Leave the rest
        And worry about it no more
Leave the door open a little
The wall can crumble
You still will have angels to guide you
        Make way to peek out
        In case you are lost
        A glimmer of hope to see
A wave of expression will follow you there
Make room for the journey to start
Little by little you will learn
To open up your heart

Kindness abounds in a sea of grace
Little things will count
A world of love
A mind of hope
Connect what once was lost

Return to the now
Poke around and grab it with both hands
Get up and go
The world awaits
For you

In this...
	Race For Time.

UP TO THE SKY

Up To The Sky
Transcend your thoughts outward
Up to the sky
Swirling and mixing with God's love
And all those that have passed before you
Gather up momentum
In all that you do
Treat others kindly and see it through
Find a way to care
If only for an instant and know that you are there for a reason.
Climb even higher
Up to the sky
Rays of sunshine propel you
Until you can fly
Free in the moment, flitting about
Dreaming and scheming in thoughts and ideas
Until you retrieve it from clouds up above
Then slowly descending, making your way carefully down
Until you connect with your feet on the ground.
What to do when you get there?
Why think little one, we have work to do and that is where it's fun!
Finding common ground with someone else to share
Your life is a myriad of stairs
At every platform, you stop and stare out
Shout your excitement and slowly ascend
To the next level of transcendence
Making your mark along the way
New hope, new ideas, a whizzing, a blurring
Connecting at each step along the path
Pause to consider, another twist and a turn

You are on your way to a tither
Return to the moment, fulfilled and excited
Ready to share your new life
Break out of the mold, see what needs to be done
And get going until you are out of breath
Twirl around and dance, sing joyous praise for the moment will
soon be gone
As you reach the top level, you are petering out
Teetering right on the edge
Until you slip over and find yourself falling
Up, up, Up To The Sky.

THE NEWNESS OF TOMORROW

The newness of tomorrow
Let me bring you there in your dreams
Show you what you can accomplish
So you can decide which way to choose

The lightness of another day
Traveling to a new dimension
Ready for a new find
Growth and opportunity show up once again
No matter how many failures
You can try again

The hopefulness of a new start
Trying to piece it all together
Dropping that which doesn't serve your purpose
So that the light will shine again

The loveliness of the breeze in the trees
Bringing together a sense of peace
Spontaneity in its forest
Rivers babbling throughout

The wisdom to start again
To see the newness of tomorrow
To experience the light without the shadow
To feel the hope without the might
And know that love will be in sight.

INSIDE YOUR CHANGES

There comes a time when all feels right
Then you turn around
Halting, fleeing the sight
Not knowing what is right
Fighting it with all your might

Lost, with no where to go
Looking up to the sky
Perhaps you ought to try
Changes are inevitable, as one already knows
So you may as well accept it and then
See as far as you can go

Push a little harder until you reach some ground
For fear will hold you back every time until you are found
Inside your heart is chaos, do not let it show
Your mind is all a chatter
So take it very slow

Change is how you face life's hurdles
Resist too many and you will see
That falling flat is not where you want to be
Connect the changes in your heart to the outside view
And you too will come to learn that change is inside of you

Open up your floodgates and let it all renew
Recharge your thoughts until you pull through
Perhaps along the way, you will see the light
And when you proceed ahead, it will be all right.

Deep inside the recesses of your mind
Nagging thoughts arise
Come and go until you say no
Steer clear of them and go

Inside your changes...
      Climb aboard and gather your thoughts and dreams for you
      Do not allow anyone to tread on your ground,
      Lest you don't make it through.
But if you think you can do it all alone,
Think again and do not fret,
For fear is all you'll get

Find a friend, and God will send
A ship to take you there
Hop aboard and open your eyes
Peacefulness will come
Just be patient and you will bend

And when you do, be prepared
For the waves of change to start
Open your heart and try to be smart
Lean into a new way to care
Only if you dare

Inside your changes...
      You may not like it
      It's hard to let go
      So do not forget
      Return to the site
     Whenever you like
Talk to those around
For when you can't do it
Someone will abound

A hug, a smile, a tear to share
Waiting out the sea of changes
Until you can find delight in the many mazes

Change can bring about goodness
But not always in the way you want
In fact you won't see it at all
Until your great fall
And you pick yourself up
Hoping to get a new start
But the pebbles become boulders, then mountains
...too treacherous to climb
So you try again tomorrow because another chance is coming
To feel inside your changes
And know you can still make a difference
Even with all the cracks and broken pieces

THE WINDOW OF LIFE

Preparing yourself for the spaces
Looking out the window pane,
    sitting on the ledge
    waiting to live again.
Wondering if there is a chance
That someone will see you there
Hoping and praying that they will care.

Going out into the world
Sight unseen
Will I make it?
Will I even be seen?
Knowing there is a chance
To grasp the window of life
    Starting anew, fresh as a rose petal

Jump up and down,
Feel your heart pumping
Thumping with joy
Seeing all there is to see
Doing, breathing, being
    One with thee.

Running to the edge
Free as a kite
Going back now
Hold on tight
There is a window of life
If only you will grab it
See through its opaqueness
Look at the spaciousness

Dare to dream again.
For your Window of Life
    Will wait no more
      Will find you now
So you can go out the door.

Experience the meandering
Breathe in the fresh scents
Curious and delirious
Like a ripe spring day
Look up into the forest
The trees will sparkle and shine
Feel the warmth on your face
Breezes will not harm

Rejuvenate your soul
Guide your inner child
To a selfless place of freedom
And start to live again.

MESMERIZED BY THE FLAME

Crackling

A rainbow of light

Halo

    Curved with white

Look within

Star in all directions

Compressed by the air

Jump out of your soul

      A circle envisioning you to go there

Split in two

      Can't be repaired

Torn apart

Still struggling to get to the top.

Saved by the Light

          Robert Frost: "Two roads diverged in a wood and
          I...I took the one less traveled by and that has made
          all the difference."

That Flame,

    that mesmerizing flame

    showed me two paths

    two distinct shapes,

two long hauls

meant for me to choose

Choose the one

    Shooting up and out

      Or one going back home.

Trying to find a way out.

The flame kept me focused and alive.

Brought me to the here and now.

Helped me to see there is light --- saved by this light.

A lot more to give.

    Became a wife, a mother, a friend. Had two daughters –
    thank God.

    Learned to love again.

Life-changing

    Light emitting

    Hope in small doses

What did those families do after 9/11?

Horrific losses

Still cannot grasp the immensity of it.

So tragically sad.

Did those children move on?

Did those wives pick up the pieces?

How did they heal?

How long is the haul?

Does the road keep on going for them?

Or does it stop in a dead end?

Will they turn around?

    Back up?

    Move out?

    Or simply charge ahead?

    Wow, what a sight.

How do they decide?

That emptiness is truly immense.

One minute leads into the next.

You are simply depleted.

No more light in your soul.

No illumination within.

No sound without

    breaking the barriers

    of life into a

    dead stillness

Choking the air right out of your head

Catch up to this

Turn it around.

Find your soul's purpose.

Try to take charge.

Illuminated path with a fork in the road.

Strain to see far ahead.

Making you choose.

> The well-trodden path or the barely concealed one.

> Robert Frost said to take the lesser of the two.

I did. I stayed.

And I WILL make a difference.

ABOUT THE AUTHOR

This work is a collection of original poetry by Karen Langran. Her poetry is designed to help anyone who has experienced severe trauma. Perhaps it will help someone work through and express their own self by finding the courage to feel and shine again.

Karen Langran, a new author, has always loved to write and has journaled since a young girl. Her motto is "When in doubt, writing gets it out." This is a work to express just that. Her hope is that if she can help just one "Split-Soul" like someone did for her, she would feel accomplished and be proud.

Karen Langran was born and raised in Rochester, New York and now resides in Arizona with her family.